Contents

Why Teach Handwriting?

Handwriting is still an important life skill. Writing by hand ties in closely with the skills of reading and comprehending. Handwriting personalizes communication with others in a way that technological devices cannot. Neat, legible writing is a skill that students can take pride in throughout their lives.

Cursive Writing Teaching Tips

- Teach in small groups of Modelled Cursive Writing sessions.
- Point out that, in cursive writing, there is usually a beginning "tail," and an ending "tail." These "tails" are what join the letters of a word together.
- Demonstrate for students how, during cursive writing, the pencil should not be lifted from the paper until the word has been completed. Only a few letters, such as capital "T," do not connect to the rest of a word when cursive writing.
- On chart paper or whiteboard, demonstrate the formation of the cursive letter being taught in writing. Describe your movements out loud as you write. Focus on the proper alignment, shape, and slant of your writing.
- Invite students to "write" the letter in the air with big arm movements.
- As students are practising their cursive writing skills, make sure to reinforce good posture habits. Slouching will create unnecessary strain on students' young spines.
- Play classical music to create an inspiring atmosphere as students practise their cursive writing skills.

Motivation

Consider these ideas to motivate students to practise their cursive writing skills, see progress, feel pride in accomplishment, and have a product to show for their hard work:

- Keep students' work organized in a portfolio, folder, or scrapbook, or bind practice pages into a book for each student.
- As students complete cursive writing lessons successfully, have them colour in their personal completion chart provided in this resource.
- For proficient cursive writers, provide short poems and nursery rhymes to copy. Encourage students to illustrate their pages and bind them together to make a book.

General Support

The classroom environment, and your attention to individual needs, can promote the development of good handwriting. Here are some tips and suggestions for helping students learn to write legibly:

- Display the cursive alphabet in the classroom where all students can see it. Consider attaching photocopies of the alphabet, with letter formation, to desks or tables for students who may need it.
- Model legible writing at every opportunity.
- Remind students to hold their writing tools properly.
- Ensure that pencils are sharpened before use.

Suggested Cursive Writing Learning Order

Teach letters with a similar formation in clusters. For example,

a c d g
h k
e f l
i j t
r s u w
b o v
m n x
p q y z

Cursive Writing Tips

Proper Posture

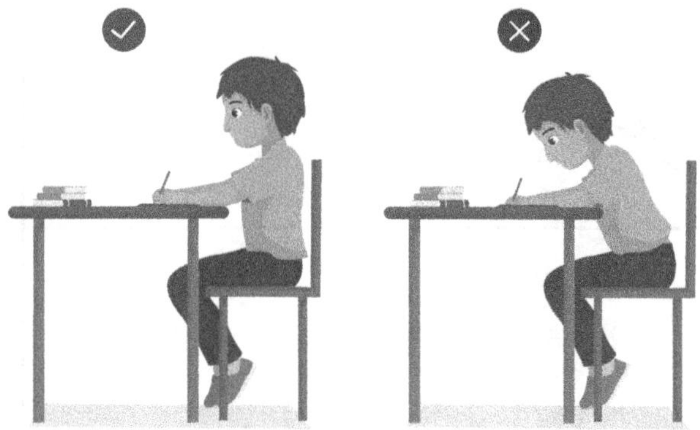

1. Keep your shoulders relaxed.

2. Keep your feet on the floor.

Paper Position

Left Handed Right Handed

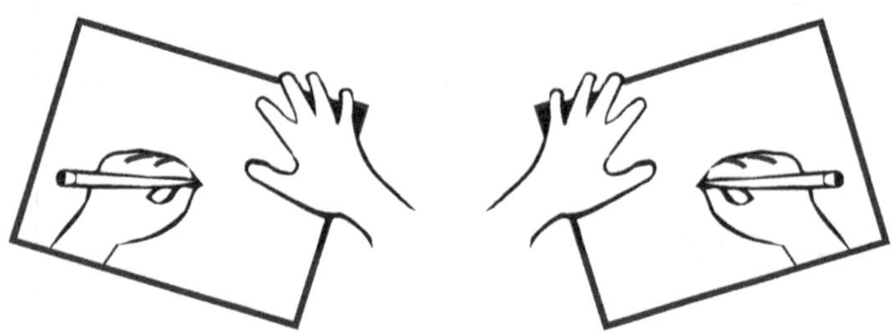

1. The paper is positioned slightly to the left (for right-handers).

2. The paper is positioned slightly to the right (for left-handers).

Pencil Grip

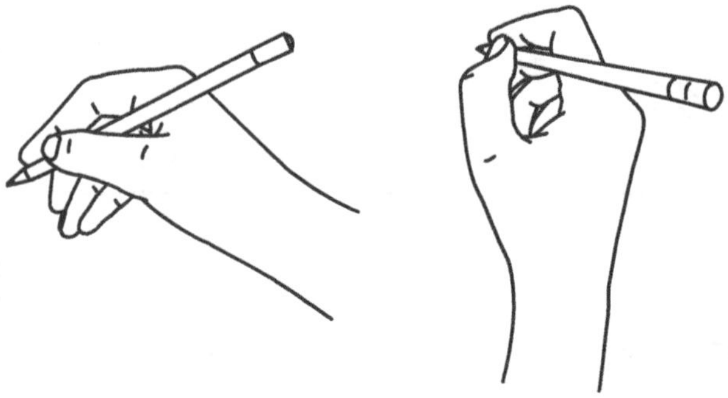

1. Keep a soft and comfortable grip.

2. Don't apply too much pressure.

Cursive Writing Progress Chart

Aa Bb Cc Dd Ee

Ff Gg Hh Ii Jj

Kk Ll Mm Nn Oo

Pp Qq Rr Ss Tt

Uu Vv Ww Xx Yy

Zz

After each cursive writing session, colour the letter(s) you completed in the chart.

Cursive Alphabet - Lowercase Letters

TRACE THE LOWERCASE LETTERS.

Cursive Alphabet - Uppercase Letters

TRACE THE UPPERCASE LETTERS.

TRACE AND WRITE.
CIRCLE YOUR BEST A OR a ON EACH LINE.

A A A A A A A A

A

A

a a a a a a a a a

a

a

act

aunt

a b c d e f g h i j k l m n o p q
r s t u v w x y z

TRACE AND WRITE.

CIRCLE YOUR BEST A OR a ON EACH LINE.

A A A A A A A A A A

A

A

a a a a a a a a a a

a

a

all

ace

a b c d e f g h i j k l m n o p q

r s t u v w x y z

TRACE AND WRITE.

CIRCLE YOUR BEST B OR b ON EACH LINE.

bar

bed

a b c d e f g h i j k l m n o p q
r s t u v w x y z

B b

TRACE AND WRITE.
CIRCLE YOUR BEST B OR b ON EACH LINE.

B B B B B B B B B

b b b b b b b b b b b

bite

bud

a b c d e f g h i j k l m n o p q
r s t u v w x y z

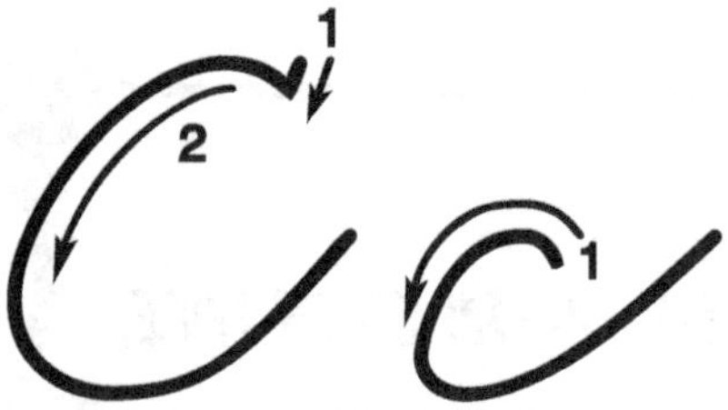

TRACE AND WRITE.
CIRCLE YOUR BEST C OR c ON EACH LINE.

cat

cod

a b c d e f g h i j k l m n o p q
r s t u v w x y z

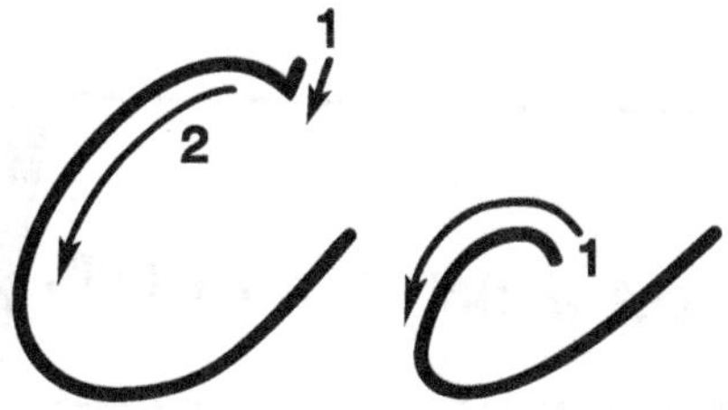

TRACE AND WRITE.
CIRCLE YOUR BEST C OR c ON EACH LINE.

cut

coat

a b c d e f g h i j k l m n o p q
r s t u v w x y z

TRACE AND WRITE.
CIRCLE YOUR BEST *D* OR *d* ON EACH LINE.

D D D D D D D D

d d d d d d d d d

dad

dew

a b c d e f g h i j k l m n o p q
r s t u v w x y z

TRACE AND WRITE.
CIRCLE YOUR BEST D OR d ON EACH LINE.

dip

doe

a b c d e f g h i j k l m n o p q
r s t u v w x y z

TRACE AND WRITE.
CIRCLE YOUR BEST E OR e ON EACH LINE.

end

eel

a b c d e f g h i j k l m n o p q
r s t u v w x y z

TRACE AND WRITE.
CIRCLE YOUR BEST ℰ OR e ON EACH LINE.

easy

egg

a b c d e f g h i j k l m n o p q
r s t u v w x y z

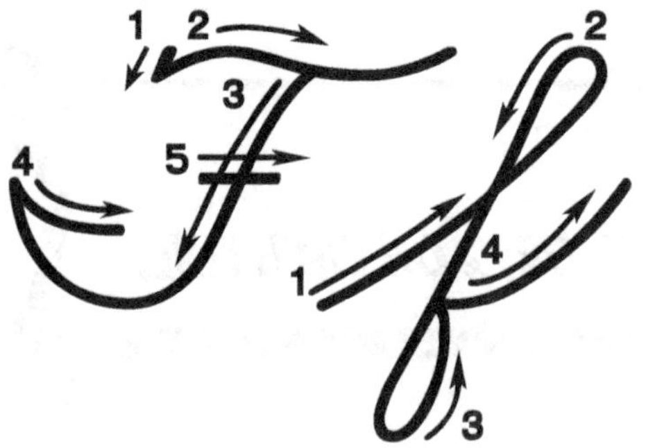

TRACE AND WRITE.
CIRCLE YOUR BEST *F* OR *f* ON EACH LINE.

fat

fed

a b c d e f g h i j k l m n o p q
r s t u v w x y z

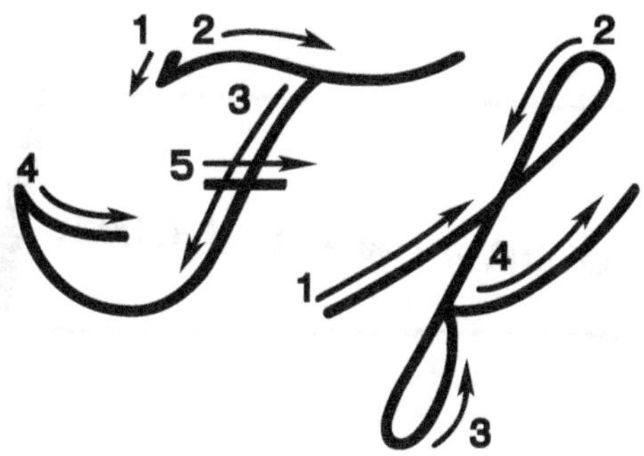

TRACE AND WRITE.
CIRCLE YOUR BEST F OR f ON EACH LINE.

fig

fog

a b c d e f g h i j k l m n o p q
r s t u v w x y z

TRACE AND WRITE.
CIRCLE YOUR BEST G OR g ON EACH LINE.

glow

gate

a b c d e f g h i j k l m n o p q
r s t u v w x y z

TRACE AND WRITE.

CIRCLE YOUR BEST G OR g ON EACH LINE.

goat

girl

a b c d e f g h i j k l m n o p q

r s t u v w x y z

TRACE AND WRITE.
CIRCLE YOUR BEST H OR h ON EACH LINE.

has

hit

a b c d e f g h i j k l m n o p q
r s t u v w x y z

TRACE AND WRITE.
CIRCLE YOUR BEST *H* OR *h* ON EACH LINE.

hope

hay

a b c d e f g h i j k l m n o p q
r s t u v w x y z

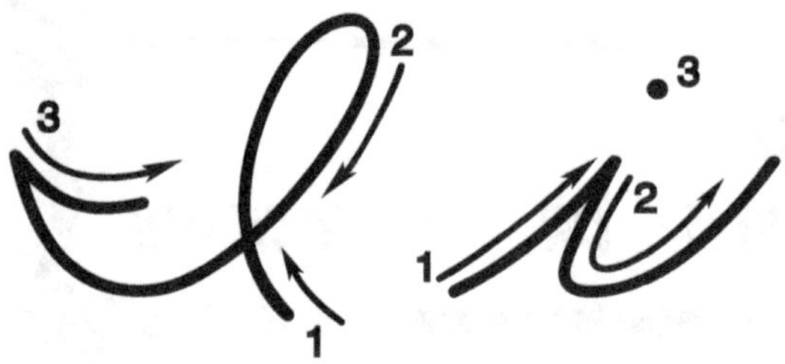

TRACE AND WRITE.
CIRCLE YOUR BEST I OR i ON EACH LINE.

into

icing

a b c d e f g h i j k l m n o p q
r s t u v w x y z

TRACE AND WRITE.
CIRCLE YOUR BEST I OR i ON EACH LINE.

idea

is

a b c d e f g h i j k l m n o p q
r s t u v w x y z

TRACE AND WRITE.
CIRCLE YOUR BEST J OR j ON EACH LINE.

jam

join

a b c d e f g h i j k l m n o p q
r s t u v w x y z

TRACE AND WRITE.

CIRCLE YOUR BEST J OR j ON EACH LINE.

jelly

jump

a b c d e f g h i j k l m n o p q
r s t u v w x y z

K k

TRACE AND WRITE.

CIRCLE YOUR BEST K OR k ON EACH LINE.

K K K K K K K K K

K

K

k k k k k k k k

k

k

keep

knit

a b c d e f g h i j k l m n o p q
r s t u v w x y z

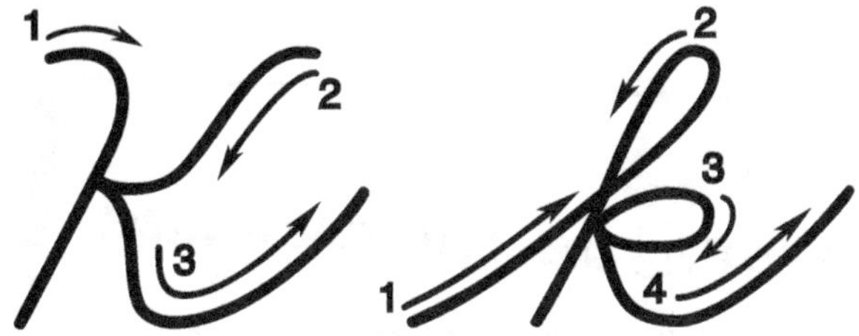

TRACE AND WRITE.
CIRCLE YOUR BEST K OR k ON EACH LINE.

K K K K K K K K K K

K

K

k k k k k k k k k

k

k

kite

koala

a b c d e f g h i j k l m n o p q
r s t u v w x y z

TRACE AND WRITE.
CIRCLE YOUR BEST *L* OR *l* ON EACH LINE.

led

load

a b c d e f g h i j k l m n o p q
r s t u v w x y z

TRACE AND WRITE.
CIRCLE YOUR BEST L OR l ON EACH LINE.

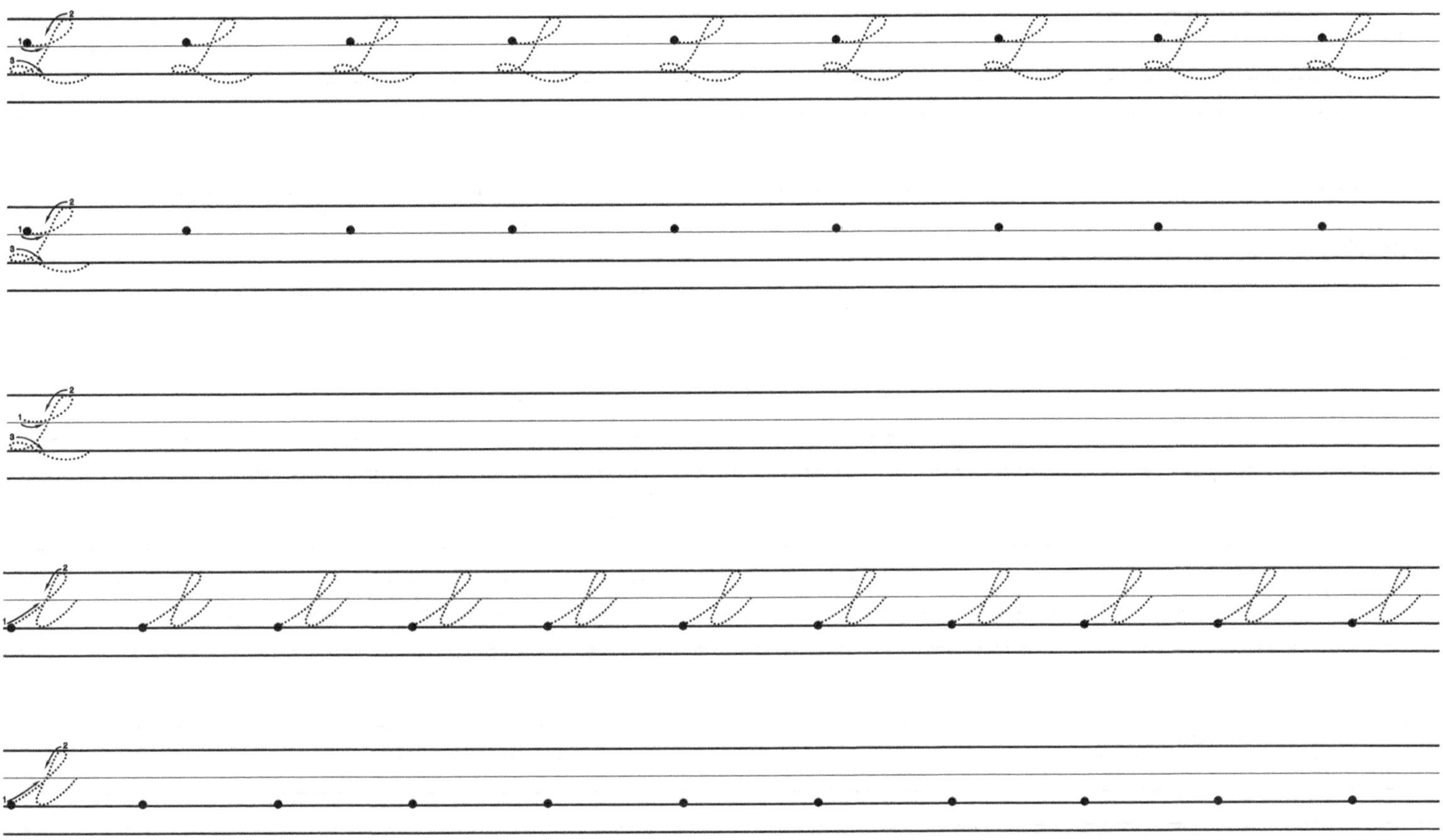

lute

lion

a b c d e f g h i j k l m n o p q
r s t u v w x y z

M m

TRACE AND WRITE.
CIRCLE YOUR BEST M OR m ON EACH LINE.

met

mom

a b c d e f g h i j k l m n o p q r s t u v w x y z

TRACE AND WRITE.

CIRCLE YOUR BEST *M* OR *m* ON EACH LINE.

mule

may

a b c d e f g h i j k l m n o p q r s t u v w x y z

N n

TRACE AND WRITE.
CIRCLE YOUR BEST N OR n ON EACH LINE.

N N N N N N N

N

N

n n n n n n n n

n

n

neat

nod

a b c d e f g h i j k l m n o p q
r s t u v w x y z

TRACE AND WRITE.
CIRCLE YOUR BEST N OR n ON EACH LINE.

nine

note

a b c d e f g h i j k l m n o p q
r s t u v w x y z

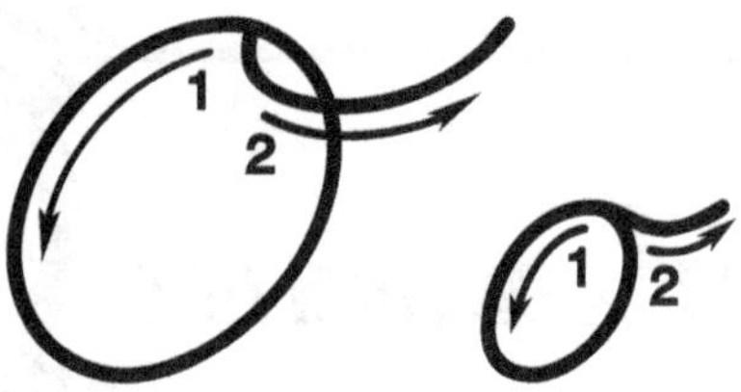

TRACE AND WRITE.
CIRCLE YOUR BEST O OR o ON EACH LINE.

oat

odd

a b c d e f g h i j k l m n o p q
r s t u v w x y z

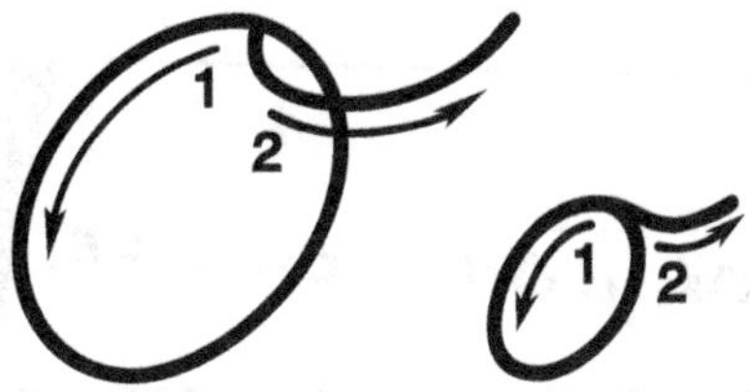

TRACE AND WRITE.
CIRCLE YOUR BEST O OR o ON EACH LINE.

oil

out

a b c d e f g h i j k l m n o p q
r s t u v w x y z

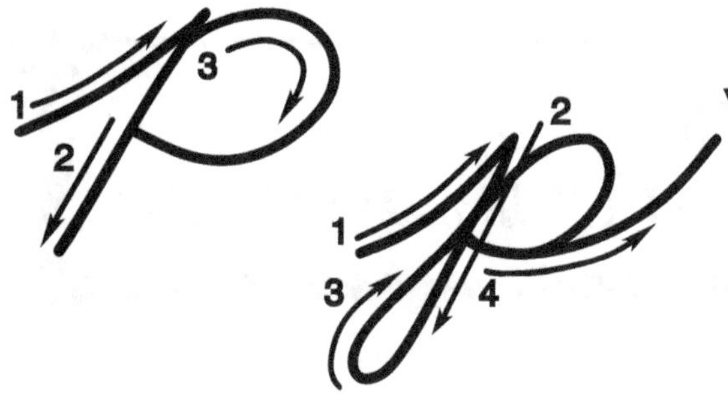

TRACE AND WRITE.
CIRCLE YOUR BEST P OR p ON EACH LINE.

pat

pine

a b c d e f g h i j k l m n o p q
r s t u v w x y z

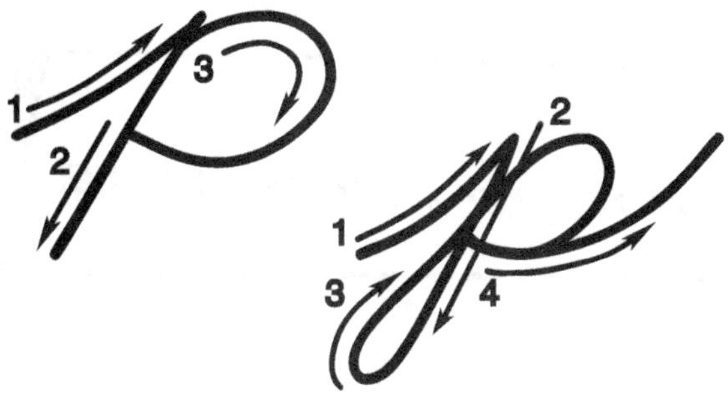

TRACE AND WRITE.
CIRCLE YOUR BEST P OR p ON EACH LINE.

poppy

pupil

a b c d e f g h i j k l m n o p q
r s t u v w x y z

TRACE AND WRITE.
CIRCLE YOUR BEST Q OR q ON EACH LINE.

Q Q Q Q Q Q Q Q

q q q q q q q q q

quill

quote

a b c d e f g h i j k l m n o p q
r s t u v w x y z

Q q

TRACE AND WRITE.
CIRCLE YOUR BEST *Q* OR *q* ON EACH LINE.

quake

quiet

a b c d e f g h i j k l m n o p q r s t u v w x y z

TRACE AND WRITE.
CIRCLE YOUR BEST R OR r ON EACH LINE.

R R R R R R R R

r r r r r r r r

ram

rock

a b c d e f g h i j k l m n o p q
r s t u v w x y z

TRACE AND WRITE.
CIRCLE YOUR BEST R OR r ON EACH LINE.

R R R R R R R R R R

R

R

r r r r r r r r r r

r

r

rare

ruler

a b c d e f g h i j k l m n o p q
r s t u v w x y z

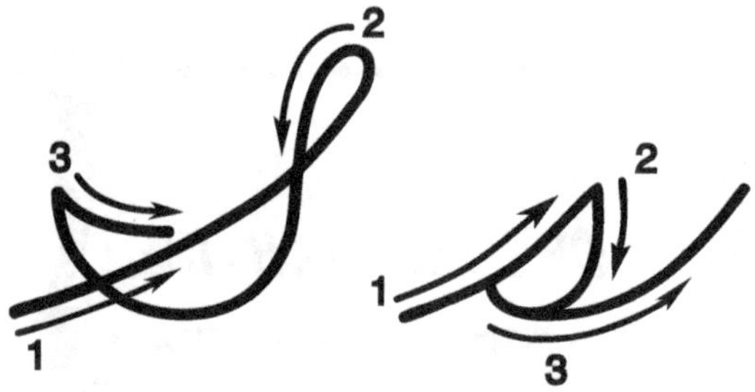

TRACE AND WRITE.
CIRCLE YOUR BEST S OR s ON EACH LINE.

sock

sister

a b c d e f g h i j k l m n o p q
r s t u v w x y z

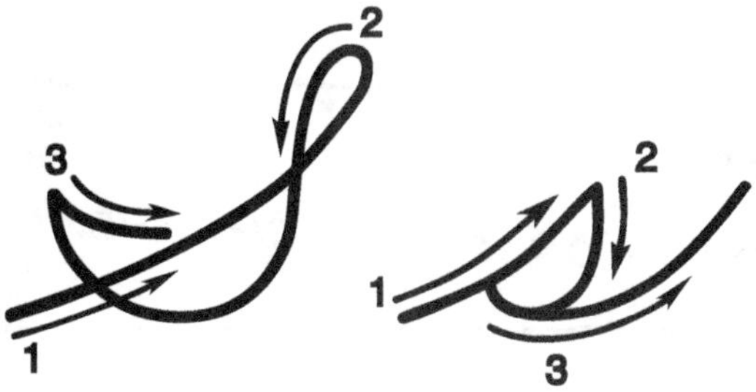

TRACE AND WRITE.
CIRCLE YOUR BEST S OR s ON EACH LINE.

sugar

salt

a b c d e f g h i j k l m n o p q
r s t u v w x y z

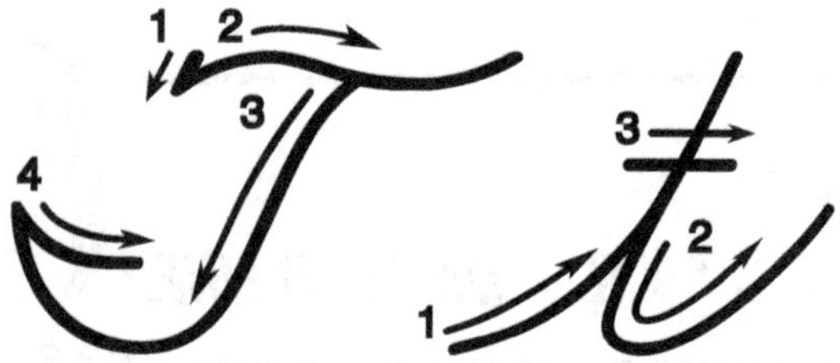

TRACE AND WRITE.
CIRCLE YOUR BEST T OR t ON EACH LINE.

T T T T T T T T

T

T

t t t t t t t t t

t

t

tent

that

a b c d e f g h i j k l m n o p q
r s t u v w x y z

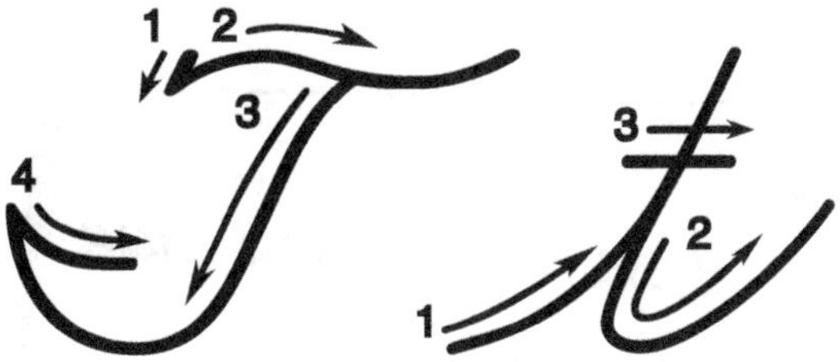

TRACE AND WRITE.
CIRCLE YOUR BEST T OR t ON EACH LINE.

true

time

a b c d e f g h i j k l m n o p q
r s t u v w x y z

TRACE AND WRITE.
CIRCLE YOUR BEST U OR u ON EACH LINE.

U U U U U U U U U

U

U

u u u u u u u

u

u

undo

upon

a b c d e f g h i j k l m n o p q
r s t u v w x y z

U u

TRACE AND WRITE.
CIRCLE YOUR BEST U OR u ON EACH LINE.

U U U U U U U U U U U

U

U

u u u u u u u u u

u

u

usual

utter

a b c d e f g h i j k l m n o p q
r s t u v w x y z

TRACE AND WRITE.
CIRCLE YOUR BEST V OR v ON EACH LINE.

very

visit

a b c d e f g h i j k l m n o p q
r s t u v w x y z

V v

TRACE AND WRITE.
CIRCLE YOUR BEST V OR v ON EACH LINE.

V V V V V V V V V V

V

V

v v v v v v v v v v v

v

v

vase

vote

a b c d e f g h i j k l m n o p q
r s t u v w x y z

W w

TRACE AND WRITE.
CIRCLE YOUR BEST W OR w ON EACH LINE.

where

wave

a b c d e f g h i j k l m n o p q r s t u v w x y z

W w

TRACE AND WRITE.
CIRCLE YOUR BEST W OR w ON EACH LINE.

W W W W W W W W W W W

W

W

w w w w w w w w w

w

w

winter

walk

a b c d e f g h i j k l m n o p q
r s t u v w x y z

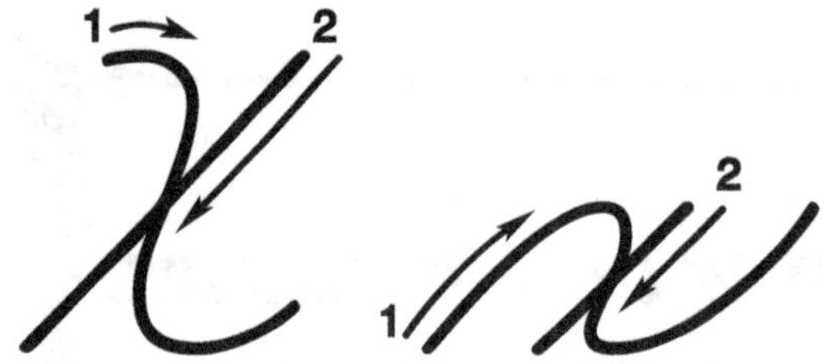

TRACE AND WRITE.
CIRCLE YOUR BEST X OR x ON EACH LINE.

X X X X X X X

x x x x x x x x x

xerox

exit

a b c d e f g h i j k l m n o p q
r s t u v w x y z

X x

TRACE AND WRITE.
CIRCLE YOUR BEST X OR x ON EACH LINE.

X X X X X X X X X

X

X

x x x x x x x x x x

x

x

xenops

xylophone

a b c d e f g h i j k l m n o p q
r s t u v w x y z

TRACE AND WRITE.
CIRCLE YOUR BEST Y OR y ON EACH LINE.

yarn

yes

a b c d e f g h i j k l m n o p q
r s t u v w x y z

TRACE AND WRITE.
CIRCLE YOUR BEST Y OR y ON EACH LINE.

yolk

yoga

a b c d e f g h i j k l m n o p q
r s t u v w x y z

TRACE AND WRITE.
CIRCLE YOUR BEST Z OR z ON EACH LINE.

zig-zag

zany

a b c d e f g h i j k l m n o p q
r s t u v w x y z

TRACE AND WRITE.
CIRCLE YOUR BEST Z OR z ON EACH LINE.

zeal

zone

a b c d e f g h i j k l m n o p q
r s t u v w x y z

Joining Letters - ai, ar, and au

PRACTISE WRITING THE JOINING LETTERS. *ai*

ai

trail

jail

PRACTISE WRITING THE JOINING LETTERS. *ar*

ar

barn

yarn

PRACTISE WRITING THE JOINING LETTERS. *au*

au

autumn

sauce

Joining Letters - aw, er, and ew

PRACTISE WRITING THE JOINING LETTERS. aw

aw

awesome

away

PRACTISE WRITING THE JOINING LETTERS. er

er

never

better

PRACTISE WRITING THE JOINING LETTERS. ew

ew

curfew

nephew

Joining Letters - ck, ch, and ir

PRACTISE WRITING THE JOINING LETTERS. ck

ck

black

snack

PRACTISE WRITING THE JOINING LETTERS. ch

ch

child

chain

PRACTISE WRITING THE JOINING LETTERS. ir

ir

spirit

stairs

Joining Letters - kn, qu, and ur

PRACTISE WRITING THE JOINING LETTERS. kn

kn

knight

know

PRACTISE WRITING THE JOINING LETTERS. qu

qu

queen

quilt

PRACTISE WRITING THE JOINING LETTERS. ur

ur

purse

turn

Joining Letters - ff, ll, and sh

Practise writing the joining letters. ff

ff

office

cliff

Practise writing the joining letters. ll

ll

well

spell

Practise writing the joining letters. sh

sh

sharp

cash

Joining Letters - th, as, and ea

PRACTISE WRITING THE JOINING LETTERS. *th*

th

think

path

PRACTISE WRITING THE JOINING LETTERS. *as*

as

basket

last

PRACTISE WRITING THE JOINING LETTERS. *ea*

ea

treat

seal

Joining Letters - ed, igh, and ing

PRACTISE WRITING THE JOINING LETTERS. *ed*

ed

packed

fled

PRACTISE WRITING THE JOINING LETTERS. *igh*

igh

light

sigh

PRACTISE WRITING THE JOINING LETTERS. *ing*

ing

trying

bring

Joining Letters - ng, squ, and ss

PRACTISE WRITING THE JOINING LETTERS. ng

ng

long

hang

PRACTISE WRITING THE JOINING LETTERS. squ

squ

squeeze

squash

PRACTISE WRITING THE JOINING LETTERS. ss

ss

massive

passing

Joining Letters - ae, be, and de

PRACTISE WRITING THE JOINING LETTERS. ae

ae

algae

aerobic

PRACTISE WRITING THE JOINING LETTERS. be

be

beach

belt

PRACTISE WRITING THE JOINING LETTERS. de

de

detail

denim

Joining Letters - ee, fe, and ge

PRACTISE WRITING THE JOINING LETTERS. ee

ee

cheese

sneeze

PRACTISE WRITING THE JOINING LETTERS. fe

fe

feast

felt

PRACTISE WRITING THE JOINING LETTERS. ge

ge

genie

germs

Joining Letters - ie, pe, and se

Practise writing the joining letters. *ie*

ie

movie

review

Practise writing the joining letters. *pe*

pe

pedal

person

Practise writing the joining letters. *se*

se

seal

insect

Joining Letters - ue, ov, and ow

Practise writing the joining letters. ue

ue

argue

guess

Practise writing the joining letters. ov

ov

oval

over

Practise writing the joining letters. ow

ow

down

tower

Joining Letters - oe, re, and ve

Practise writing the joining letters. oe

oe

goes

foe

Practise writing the joining letters. re

re

reach

rental

Practise writing the joining letters. ve

ve

venue

vertical

Joining Letters - we, ere, and ure

PRACTISE WRITING THE JOINING LETTERS. we

we

weigh

weekend

PRACTISE WRITING THE JOINING LETTERS. ere

ere

there

nowhere

PRACTISE WRITING THE JOINING LETTERS. ure

ure

pure

sure

Joining Letters - oa, oi, and oo

PRACTISE WRITING THE JOINING LETTERS. oa

oa

float

coach

PRACTISE WRITING THE JOINING LETTERS. oi

oi

boil

choice

PRACTISE WRITING THE JOINING LETTERS. oo

oo

moon

cartoon

Joining Letters - op, or, and ou

PRACTISE WRITING THE JOINING LETTERS. op

op

open

optic

PRACTISE WRITING THE JOINING LETTERS. or

or

organ

forward

PRACTISE WRITING THE JOINING LETTERS. ou

ou

outside

about

Number Words

one

two

three

four

five

six

seven

eight

nine

ten

Number Words (cont.)

eleven

twelve

thirteen

fourteen

fifteen

sixteen

seventeen

eighteen

nineteen

twenty

Number Words (cont.)

thirty

forty

fifty

sixty

seventy

eighty

ninety

hundred

thousand

million

billion

Days of the Week

Monday

Tuesday

Wednesday

Thursday

Friday

Saturday

Sunday

Months of the Year

January

February

March

April

May

June

Months of the Year (cont.)

July

August

September

October

November

December

Seasons of the Year

TRACE AND WRITE EACH SEASON WORD.
WRITE A LIST OF ACTIVITIES YOU LIKE TO DO FOR EACH SEASON.

spring

summer

autumn

winter

Inspirational Quotes

PRACTISE WRITING EACH SENTENCE.

You can do more than you think.

Don't ignore your own potential.

Trust your crazy ideas.

You can change the world.

Be the reason someone smiles.

Inspirational Quotes (cont.)

PRACTISE WRITING EACH SENTENCE.

Remember to believe in yourself.

Positive vibes only.

Be the change you wish to see.

Fall seven times, stand up eight.

Your uniqueness makes you shine.

Inspirational Quotes (cont.)

PRACTISE WRITING EACH SENTENCE.

Even the greatest were beginners.

Worry is a misuse of imagination.

Appreciate the moment.

Kind words cost nothing.

Embrace your inner superhero.

Inspirational Quotes (cont.)

PRACTISE WRITING EACH SENTENCE.

Let your differences shine.

No storm can last forever.

Don't sweat the small stuff.

A watched pot never boils.

Everyday is a second chance.

Proverbs & Sayings

PRACTISE WRITING EACH SENTENCE.

The early bird catches the worm.

Strike while the iron is hot.

A penny saved is a penny earned.

A stitch in time saves nine.

Honesty is the best policy.

Proverbs & Sayings (cont.)

PRACTISE WRITING EACH SENTENCE.

Curiosity killed the cat.

It's the tip of the iceberg.

It's better to be safe than sorry.

A leopard doesn't change its spots.

All is well that ends well.

Proverbs & Sayings (cont.)

PRACTISE WRITING EACH SENTENCE.

It takes two to tango.

All that glitters is not gold.

All good things come to an end.

Empty bags can't stand upright.

Laughter is the best medicine.

Proverbs & Sayings (cont.)

PRACTISE WRITING EACH SENTENCE.

Every cloud has a silver lining.

Practice makes perfect.

Money doesn't grow on trees.

It's not over till it's over.

The squeaky wheel gets the grease.

Jokes

PRACTISE WRITING EACH JOKE.

What do you call a fake noodle?

An impasta!

What do cats eat for breakfast?

Mice Crispies!

Jokes (cont.)

Practise writing each joke.

What does a triceratops sit on?

Its tricera-bottom!

Why can't you trust tacos?

They always spill the beans!

Jokes (cont.)

Practise writing each joke.

Why was the math book sad?

It had too many problems!

Why are ghosts bad liars?

You can see right through them!

Jokes (cont.)

PRACTISE WRITING EACH JOKE.

Why is grass so dangerous?

Because it's full of blades!

Why are elevator jokes so good?

They work on many levels!

Read All About Me!

My name is...

My Portrait...

I live...

All about my family...

Read All About Me!

My age is...

My birthday is in...

I am in grade...

How I like to spend my time...

My Favourites!

Colour:

Book:

Movie:

Food:

Read All About Me!

When I grow up I would like to be...

Places I would like to visit are...

My favourite joke is...

Cursive Writing Challenges

Colour in the box as you complete a cursive writing challenge.

Copy your favourite poem.	Copy the lyrics to one of your favourite songs.	Write a thank you note.
Copy a recipe.	Create an invitation to an event.	Copy five proverbs or sayings.
Copy some of your favourite jokes.	Make a list of your favourite books.	Write a letter to a friend or relative.
Make a grocery list.	Copy five riddles you enjoy.	Copy the rules of a game.

Write a Letter

Practise Your Signature

Collect Signatures

Writing Prompt: Tech-Savvy Genie

You are granted three wishes by a tech-savvy genie who emerges from a smartphone. What do you wish for, and what are the unexpected consequences?

☐ *I checked for spelling and punctuation.* ☐ *My writing makes sense.*

Writing Prompt: The Ultimate Vacation

Describe your ultimate vacation. What makes it amazing? Dive into every sensory detail, from the sights and sounds to the tastes and textures.

☐ I checked for spelling and punctuation. ☐ My writing makes sense.

Writing Prompt: Finish What You Start

How important is it to finish what you start?
Provide examples from your own life or famous figures
who have shown this trait.

☐ *I checked for spelling and punctuation.* ☐ *My writing makes sense.*

Writing Prompt: Mobile Devices in Class

Should students be allowed to bring their mobile devices to class? Make a case for or against this idea, providing specific reasons and benefits or drawbacks.

☐ *I checked for spelling and punctuation.* ☐ *My writing makes sense.*

Writing Prompt: Meeting Someone Famous

If you could meet any famous person, who would it be and why? What would you ask them, and how do you think they would respond?

☐ *I checked for spelling and punctuation.* ☐ *My writing makes sense.*

Writing Prompt: $1,000,000

You suddenly find yourself the owner of $1,000,000. What will you do with it? Include at least one twist no one would see coming.

☐ *I checked for spelling and punctuation.* ☐ *My writing makes sense.*

Writing Prompt: Time Travelling

If given a chance, would you travel to the past or the future? Explain your choice, the exact time period you would visit, and what you hope to learn or change.

☐ I checked for spelling and punctuation. ☐ My writing makes sense.

Writing Prompt: One Food For a Week

If you had to eat only one food for an entire week, what would it be and why? Describe the food in detail and how you think you would feel by the end of the week.

☐ *I checked for spelling and punctuation.* ☐ *My writing makes sense.*

Writing Prompt: Dream Job

What's your dream job? Explain why you are drawn to it, the impact you hope to have, and the journey you anticipate taking to get there.

☐ *I checked for spelling and punctuation.* ☐ *My writing makes sense.*

Writing Prompt: A Hidden World

Imagine discovering a hidden world in the heart of your city. What's it like? Describe the hidden world in detail.

☐ I checked for spelling and punctuation. ☐ My writing makes sense.

Writing Prompt: 50 Years From Now

Imagine you have a time machine that takes you forward 50 years. That's 50 years from now! What do you think the world will look like? How will people live, play, work, and learn?

☐ I checked for spelling and punctuation. ☐ My writing makes sense.

Superheroes Among Us

Superheroes aren't just in movies or comics. They are everyday people who help others. Think of firefighters, doctors, or even a neighbour who helps everyone. They may not wear capes, but they make the world a better place!

1. Who is your real-life superhero and why?

2. What kind of superhero would you like to be?

All About Bees

Often celebrated for their honey-making skills, bees are environmental superheroes with a much more crucial task: pollination. These small but mighty creatures dart from flower to flower, transferring pollen and ensuring that plants can produce the fruits and vegetables we enjoy every day. However, bees are in peril due to factors like pesticides, habitat loss, and climate change, leading to dire consequences for global food production and natural ecosystems. The survival of bees is intricately tied to biodiversity and the health of the planet, making their protection an urgent issue that calls for immediate action from all of us.

1. Why are bees important for us and our food?

Music to My Ears

Music is a universal language. Whether it's pop, rock, country, rap, classical, or jazz, it makes us feel different emotions. Instruments like drums, guitars, or violins help create music. Even your own voice can be an instrument!

1. What's your favourite type of music and why?

2. If you could learn any instrument, which one would it be?

3. How does music make you feel?

Physical Exercise

Physical exercise isn't just about building muscles or endurance; it's a key ingredient for a happy, healthy life. Regular physical activity strengthens the heart, improves lung function, and can help prevent serious health issues like diabetes and heart disease. But the benefits don't stop with physical health. Exercise acts as a natural mood booster by releasing endorphins, often referred to as 'feel-good' hormones, which reduce feelings of stress and anxiety. Whether it's a brisk walk, a dance class, or a friendly game of soccer, staying active is essential for both body and mind, enhancing overall quality of life and well-being.

1. Explain how regular physical activity contributes to maintaining a healthy body and preventing various health issues.

Cursive Writing Rubric

Name: ______________________________ **Date:** ____________________

	Emergent	Developing	Capable	Mastered
Letter Shape	Few letters are formed correctly.	Some letters are formed correctly.	Most of the letters are formed correctly.	Almost all letters are formed correctly.
Slant of Letters	Little uniformity in slant of letters.	Some uniformity in slant of letters.	Good uniformity in slant of letters.	Excellent uniformity in slant of letters.
Connection to the Line	Few letters are within the lines.	Some letters are within the lines.	Most letters are within the lines.	Almost all letters are within the lines.
Letter Spacing	Few letters are spaced appropriately.	Some letters are spaced appropriately.	Most letters are spaced appropriately.	Almost all letters are spaced appropriately.
Neatness	Few letters/ words are legible.	Some letters/ words are legible.	Most letters/ words are legible.	Almost all letters/ words are legible.
Daily Work	Cursive writing skills learned are rarely applied to daily work.	Cursive writing skills learned are sometimes applied to daily work.	Cursive writing skills learned are usually applied to daily work.	Cursive writing skills learned are consistently applied to daily work.

Observations:

____

____

____

Letters Requiring Practice:

Cursive Handwriting Certificate of Completion

Signature

Great Work!